A Reader's
Theater Script
and
Guide

一看京
少儿英语小剧场

有趣的节日

主　编　杜效明
副主编　闵　璇
编　委　潘晨曦　凌　凝　杨德俊　周莹莹　张玉霞
　　　　张文慧　慕媛媛　吴　昊　赵　芹　吴秀玲
　　　　冯　会　余晓琴　都兰芳

ART TIME
时代出版
时代出版传媒股份有限公司
安徽科学技术出版社

图书在版编目（CIP）数据

有趣的节日 / 杜效明主编.--合肥:安徽科学技术出版社,2022.1
（一看就会演的少儿英语小剧场）
ISBN 978-7-5337-8464-5

Ⅰ.①有…　Ⅱ.①杜…　Ⅲ.①英语-少儿读物
Ⅳ.①H319.4

中国版本图书馆 CIP 数据核字(2021)第 123019 号

YOUQU DE JIERI

有 趣 的 节 日

主　编　杜效明

副主编　闵　璇

出 版 人：丁凌云　　选题策划：张　雯　周璟瑜　　责任编辑：周璟瑜
责任校对：张　枫　　责任印制：廖小青　　装帧设计：武　迪
出版发行：时代出版传媒股份有限公司　http://www.press-mart.com
　　　　　安徽科学技术出版社　　　　http://www.ahstp.net
　　　　　（合肥市政务文化新区翡翠路 1118 号出版传媒广场,邮编:230071）
　　　　　电话：(0551)63533330
印　　制：合肥锦华印务有限公司　　电话：(0551)65539314
（如发现印装质量问题,影响阅读,请与印刷厂商联系调换）

开本：710×1010　1/16　　印张：6.5　　字数：130 千
版次：2022 年 1 月第 1 版　　2022 年 1 月第 1 次印刷

ISBN 978-7-5337-8464-5　　　　　　　　定价：28.00 元

推荐序

　　"一看就会演的少儿英语小剧场"系列图书是一套以英语短剧为表现形式的双语读物,选编了8个家喻户晓的童话故事,故事幽默诙谐,富有戏剧性;语言地道,童趣盎然,并提供发音纯正的音频,带来真实、生动的情境体验。

　　本系列图书集自主阅读、分角色朗读、戏剧表演等多种功能于一体,学生可以通过剧本诵读、戏剧表演和贯穿其中的互动合作,获得语言感知、语言理解、语言运用和语言鉴赏的多种体验,在语言、情感、思维、文化意识等多方面获得整体提升。

　　英语小剧场是一场由想象力构建的活动,它和普通而枯燥的死记硬背型阅读活动有本质区别。《义务教育英语课程标准》提出,小学生除了简单的听、说、读、写,还应能够进行英语表演。生动有趣的戏剧表演已成为一种以文学作品的口述演绎为中心的综合语言艺术活动。语言在戏剧中是不可或缺的元素,作家通过语言表达戏剧的立意和冲突,演员通过台词表达人物的思想和精神,导演也必须帮助演员处理台词。古希腊时期,许多知名的政治家都要拜演员为师,向演员学习台词功夫,以便提高他们的演说水平。声、台、形、表,基本功对表演艺术来说是缺一不可的,因此演员要具备声乐艺术、语言艺术、舞蹈艺术和表演艺术的修养。作为一种听、说、读、写、思全面发展的活动体验，戏剧表演对学生的英语语言学习和综合素质的提升起到了独特的作用，有助于提高学生的主动阅读能力、批判性思考能力、创意写作能力、精确表达能力、专注倾听能力以及高效的协作能力。

戏剧艺术既是综合艺术（时间和空间艺术的综合），也是集体艺术，需要集体协作才能完成。英国教育学家约翰内森和卡恩认为："运用小组协作的方式来促成学生之间更高级、更深层的互动，这一点尤其重要。"小剧场的表演形式使学生围绕着一个共同的目标进行团队协作，他们可以就内容、角色、舞台表演等细节进行充分讨论沟通。戏剧表演给学生提供了可以广泛参与的学习模式，丰富学生的实践经历，提高学生的团队合作能力。

对于教师而言，也需要一些创新、不同寻常的项目应用于课堂实践。本书中生动有趣的英语短剧，融合了极具时代感的语言表达；随书附赠的《阅读指导》手册，为教师提供具有实操性的说明和指导，帮助策划、实施并完成一场别开生面的戏剧表演活动，开展新颖有趣的第二课堂。学生们可以投入极大的热情且无须耗费太多精力，在相对较短的时间内即可产出一部成熟的舞台作品。本系列图书熔素质教育和英语教学于一炉，是小学英语教学实践的应用范例。

导读

你爱不爱做道具？有没有兴趣来画布景呢？你喜欢表演吗？如果是的话，那么就来排场话剧吧。话剧多有趣啊！话剧是让孩子们学会团队合作的最好的方法！

读者剧场的形式最简单。小读者坐在舞台的椅子上，他们不用背台词，只要把对话有感情地朗读出来便成功啦！

朗读剧场和一般的舞台剧有点儿像。演员们不仅要化装、穿戏服，还要在台上走位，一边说台词一边表演。不过，演员全程是可以看台词的。除此之外，舞台上还要搭布景、放道具。

读者剧场的台本还可以用作木偶剧。小演员站在台幕后，一边移动木偶，一边读对话。

定下话剧形式后，你首先要找到一个足够大的空间来表演。小礼堂的舞台是个不错的选择哟！当然，你也可以在教室里演出。接下来，你要初步定下演出的日期，提交使用舞台的申请。然后，为你的演出做些宣传吧。你可以把宣传单或海报张贴到学校或者社区的布告栏里。

　　别忘了把这个消息告诉朋友和家人哟！大家都会很期待你的表演的！

show出你的发音
争当英语小明星
▶ 地道口语课
▶ 剧本推荐

微信扫码

目录

英语·小·剧场
展示大舞台

show出你的发音，争当英语小明星

跟我说 ✦ **地道口语课**

实用外教口语定制课程，标准英语脱口而出

跟我听 ✦ **剧本推荐**

精听好剧本，带你"真听真看真感受"

微信扫码
还可获取本书推荐书单
好书读不停！

门票和剧目单

　　你可以亲手制作门票和剧目单，也可以用电脑设计它们。不论你选择哪种方法，一定要确定门票上标有剧名、演出日期和具体时间，以及演出地点。

　　剧目单上应列有节目顺序。剧目单的正面一般印有剧名和演出时间。演员及工作人员的姓名要放在剧目单内页。记得要准备足够的剧目单，并在开演之前把它们发给入场的观众哟。

演员和舞台工作人员

　　一场话剧需要很多人的参与。首先，让我们来分配角色。剧组的每个演员都要配有剧本，并且要熟练地掌握自己的台词。一遍遍地高声朗读你的台词可以让你更快地找到感觉。

　　接下来，需要招工作人员了。一场话剧没有这些重要的工作人员怎么行呢！一个人是可以负责多项工作的。

总导演：管理人员，布置任务。

服装设计师：借道具、做服装都是他们的工作。

舞台监督：保障每个环节顺利进行。

灯光设计师：负责打聚光灯和换光。

布景师：设计、制作布景。

道具师：筹备、制作、管理道具。

特效工作人员：负责音效和特效。

妆容和服装

　　化妆师的工作是整场演出的重中之重！每个参与的演员都是要化妆的，不过，舞台演员化的妆要比我们日常生活中化得浓一点儿。你手边要有基本的彩妆用品，比如睫毛膏、粉底液、腮红和口红等。可以用一次性化妆棉或化妆用棉签给演员上妆，要保证卫生哟！

　　服装设计师需要按照剧情设计服装。他们负责借服装，或者按照每个角色对旧衣服进行改造。借服装或者制作演出服时，你也可以向家长寻求帮助。

布景和道具

在读者剧场中，道具就是椅子，演员只需要坐在最前面就可以了。相比之下，朗读剧场和一般的舞台剧可就不是这么简单了，布景和道具是必不可少的。

布景是为每一幕布置的景物。

道具是演员在演出时需要用到的器物。

排演安排和舞台方位

一旦做出上演话剧的决定，就要制作一张彩排时间表喽，并协调大家的时间，尽量在公演之前彩排五次吧。

即便你只需要按照剧本读台词，但是，作为一个团队，你们还是要一起练习。熟练掌握自己的台词后，舞台表演才能更加流畅、自然。没有台词的时候，只要演员还留在台上，就需要做出符合自己角色的动作和表情。

剧本里的舞台方位是从演员的角度得出的，被标注在括号内。表演时，你要面向观众席，所以，左边指的就是你的左手边，右边指的就是你的右手边。

有些舞台术语可能让你摸不着头脑，比如

大幕：舞台的主要幕布，在台口内。

观众席：观众的座位。

侧幕：舞台的左、右边，是藏在观众视线之外的舞台的侧面。

故事剧场一

小幽灵和橡皮虫

布景

第一幕中，威尔画南瓜的时候，需要画笔和颜料。另外，他还需要一块抹布来清理刷子。

第二幕发生在学校外面。你需要用硬纸板做几棵光秃秃的树，也可以把几根真树权插在填满沙子的桶里或者小花盆里。在硬纸板上画好并裁出洋楼当作这一幕的舞台背景。台上还要撒些假树叶。

第三幕和第五幕的背景可有可无。如果你想为这一幕搭背景，可以用硬纸板画出房外的墙或者把类似外墙的墙纸直接贴在硬纸板上。你可以在同一块硬纸板的正反两面贴上不同颜色的墙纸，这样就做好两栋"房子"啦。

第四幕参考使用第二幕的小洋楼。隔离带可以围在房子周围，或者围在房子附近的人行道上，做出隔离一段路的效果。

道具

- □ 几个大南瓜
- □ 碗
- □ 几瓶水
- □ 画画的刷子
- □ 零食
- □ 手电筒

- □ 颜料
- □ 纸杯蛋糕
- □ 讨糖果的小袋子
- □ 抹布
- □ 曲奇饼干
- □ 杯子

演员表

詹姆士：阿莱克斯的哥哥

阿莱克斯：詹姆士的弟弟

威尔：詹姆士最要好的朋友

艾玛：男孩子们的朋友，也是同班同学

克丽斯滕：男孩子们的朋友，也是同班同学

克蕾格老师：孩子们的新班主任

妆容和服装

先前几幕，演员可以穿生活装上台表演。

万圣节当天的一幕开始，演员需要着特殊服装或配饰：

詹姆士、阿莱克斯、威尔、克丽斯滕、艾玛和克蕾格老师都需要万圣节的服装。

show出你的发音
争当英语小明星
▶ 地道口语课
▶ 剧本推荐

微信扫码

排演安排和舞台方位

右侧幕区
舞台右侧

上舞台中心
舞台正位
下舞台中心

左侧幕区
舞台左侧

Script: Ghosts and Gummy Worms

Scene 1: The Auditorium

(Will is painting a giant pumpkin. James walks on from stage right.)

James: Hey, nice pumpkin! I love Halloween!

Will: Yeah, me too. I especially love all that candy.

James: I like the spooky stories. Someday, I hope I'll see a real ghost.

Will: Not me, man. I'll pass. I don't like being scared to death.

James: Is that pumpkin for the school play?

Will: Yes, Miss Craig asked me to paint some of the props and scenery.

James: She seems super nice! Last week, she brought

kites for everyone in Alex's class. They flew them up on the hill behind the school for science class.

Will: Wow, science wasn't like that when I was in second grade!

James: I know, right? And Alex says Miss Craig never yells at her class!

Will: I wish we were that lucky. She's the first new teacher we've had in town in years!

James: I heard she moved here from California.

Will: Why would anyone move here from California?

James: Who knows! I'm just glad she did. This is the first year Alex has really liked school.

Will: *(Stops painting and looks puzzled.)* I still think it's funny that Mr. Rossi decided to retire *after* the school year began.

James: Maybe he took a look at this year's second grade class and decided to run for it! There are at least five other kids just like Alex.

Will: *(Rolling his eyes.)* Your little brother isn't *that* bad.

James: You don't live in the same house with him! Last night he put gummy worms in my bed while I was in the bathroom. I kind of shrieked when I shoved my feet down on top of them. I could hear him giggling all the way down the hall. Now every time he sees me, he squeals "Eeeeeek!" just to tease me.

Will: *(Laughing.)* Put gummy worms in his bed tonight.

James: No way. He'll just tell Mom and then *I'll* get in trouble. Are you almost done? I don't want to miss the buses. We're going to the mall tonight to get Alex a Halloween costume.

Will: What does he want to be?

James: I don't know, probably a pirate or some sort of bloodthirsty monster. Are you going to dress up when we take him trick-or-treating?

Will: I'm not sure yet. *(Pretends to clean off brush with rag.)*

James: I have a great troll mask! Do you want to borrow it?

Will: No, I think I have an idea. I just need to get a couple of things. *(Puts down his brush.)* I guess this is okay. Let's go!

剧本：小幽灵和橡皮虫

第一幕：舞台

（威尔正在画一个巨型南瓜，詹姆士从舞台右侧进入。）

詹姆士：嘿，这南瓜画得真不错哟！我太爱过万圣节了！

威尔：我也是。尤其是那些糖果，简直是我的最爱！

詹姆士：我的最爱是——那些让你起鸡皮疙瘩的故事！希望有一天，我真的能见到幽灵。

威尔：啊？这事儿可别算上我，伙计。我可不想被吓死。

詹姆士：哈哈。哎，你那个大南瓜是给学校话剧准备的吗？

威尔：对呀，克蕾格老师让我画点儿小装饰，再画点儿布景。

詹姆士：克蕾格老师看起来挺和蔼的！上周，她给阿莱克斯班里的每个人都带了风筝。那节科学课，他们一起去学校后面的山上放风筝了。

威尔：哇，当年我二年级的时候，可不是这么上科学课的！

詹姆士：我知道，朋友，咱们可没这么上过。阿莱克斯还说，克蕾格老师从来没跟他们发过火！

威尔：要是我们有他们这么幸运该多好啊！咱们镇上这么多年都没来过新老师，克蕾格老师可是第一位啊！

詹姆士：我听说她是从加利福尼亚搬过来的。

威尔：啊？竟然有人从加利福尼亚搬到这小镇来？

詹姆士：谁知道呢！总之，我特别开心她搬到这儿了。阿莱克斯说，今年他喜欢上学了。

威尔：（放下手中的笔，困惑地看着詹姆士）罗西老师开学后才决定要退休，这事儿我觉得挺有意思的。

詹姆士：也许，他是看了这届的二年级学生后，才决定退休的！这班里至少有五个像阿莱克斯那样的捣蛋鬼。

威尔：（翻白眼）你弟弟也没你说的那么糟糕啊。

詹姆士：你又不跟他住在一起，你怎么知道！昨晚我去洗漱的时候，他把橡皮虫①放在了我的床上。我一钻进被子，脚就碰到了它们，吓得我叫了起来。整个过道都能听到他咯咯的笑声。现在他每次见到我，都做出惊恐的表情，还"哎呀"地学我吓到的样子，就是要我难堪。

威尔：（大笑）那你今晚也把橡皮虫放在他床上呗。

詹姆士：算了吧。他会立马告诉妈妈，然后，我就有大麻烦了。你画完了吗？我想赶上那班公交车。我们今晚要去购物中心，给阿莱克斯买万圣节的服装。

威尔：他今年想扮什么呢？

詹姆士：不知道，估计是海盗或者嗜血怪物什么的。我们带他去要糖果的时候，你也会扮上吗？

威尔：我还不知道呢。（做出用抹布清理画笔的样子）

詹姆士：我有个超酷的魔兽面具！要不要借给你？

威尔：谢谢，不用了。我觉得，我有个好点子，只需要几样东西就可以实现了。（放下画笔）画好了。咱们走吧！

---

① 橡皮虫，也叫毛毛虫软糖，是小朋友爱吃的零食。

Scene 2: Main Street Outside the School

(James and Will enter from stage right. An old mansion painted on cardboard and surrounded by caution tape serves as the background.)

James: Look! There's yellow tape around the front of the old Miller mansion!

Will: It's probably a crime scene! Who knows what goes on in that old place.

James: When we drove past it last night on the way to get pizza, Alex swore he saw a light on downstairs.

Will: Well that's just weird. No one has lived in the Miller mansion for years.

James: *(Makes spooky noises.)* I'm surprised they haven't torn it down.

Will: Yeah, I don't want it falling on me!

James: That's what the yellow tape is for—to keep people away!

Will: *(Putting up his hands.)* They don't need tape to keep me out. You couldn't pay me to go in there!

James: That place has to be haunted.

(Miss Craig enters from stage left with Emma and Kyrsten.)

Kyrsten: Good night, Miss Craig!

Miss Craig: Good night, girls! Good night, boys! Thanks for your help with the scenery, Will!

Will: The pumpkin's finished! I'll work on the spooky tree tomorrow night.

Miss Craig: I don't need the tree until Friday afternoon, so you still have a couple of days. Thanks again. Good night! *(She exits stage right.)*

James: *(Whispering.)* There aren't any cars over there. I wonder where she parked.

Emma: Maybe someone is picking her up?

James: *(Doubtfully.)* Maybe.

Emma: My mom said I can have friends over to carve pumpkins tomorrow night. Do you guys want to come?

Will: Will there be food?

Emma: *(Laughing.)* Of course there will be food, Will! Mom's making sloppy joes and nachos for everybody.

James: Sounds good!

Kyrsten: And I'm making pumpkin cupcakes with cream cheese frosting!

Will: Even better! Count me in. What time?

Emma: Come around six o'clock. And don't forget your pumpkins!

James: I might have to bring Alex with me. Is that okay?

Emma: Sure, that's fine.

Kyrsten: See you tomorrow!

James & **Will:** Bye!

(Girls exit stage right. Boys exit stage left.)

第二幕：学校外的主干道

（詹姆士和威尔从舞台右边上台。背景为一个硬纸板做的小洋楼，洋楼被隔离带围住。）

詹姆士：你看！老米勒的洋楼前都是隔离带！

威尔：可能出事了！谁知道那个旧房子里发生了什么。

詹姆士：昨晚我们开车去买比萨，路过这栋房子时，阿莱克斯发誓，他看到楼下有光。

威尔：噢，这听起来挺怪的。米勒洋楼好多年都没有房客了。

詹姆士：（发出恐怖的声音）不可思议，这么多年都没人拆它。

威尔：对啊，它那么旧了，我可不想哪天被砸在下面。

詹姆士：这就是为什么它周围都是隔离带——让人们离这个房子远远的！

威尔：（高举双手）用不着隔离带来拦我。你付我钱，我都不愿意去呢！

詹姆士：这个地方肯定有幽灵。

（克蕾格老师、艾玛和克丽斯滕从舞台左边上台）

克丽斯滕：晚安，克蕾格老师！

克蕾格老师：再见，孩子们！威尔，谢谢你帮我做布景！

威尔：南瓜已经完工了！明晚，我会再把那棵恐怖树画完。

克蕾格老师：到周五下午，我还用不上那棵树，所以你还有几天时间呢。再次谢谢你！晚安了！（她从舞台右侧下台。）

詹姆士：（小声说）那儿一辆车也没有。我在想，她把车停在哪儿了。

艾玛：或许有人接她吧。

詹姆士：（怀疑的表情）可能吧。

艾玛：我妈妈说，明晚我可以请朋友们来家里刻南瓜。你们愿不愿意来？

威尔：有好吃的吗？

艾玛：（大笑）当然有啦，威尔！我妈会给大家准备烤玉米片和邋遢乔汉堡①。

---

① 邋遢乔汉堡是用软面包、牛肉馅、酱牛肉和芝士做的。

詹姆士：听上去不错哟！

克丽斯滕：我会给你们做奶油夹心糖衣小蛋糕！

威尔：听起来很棒！算我一个。几点呢？

艾玛：晚上六点左右吧。别忘了带上你们的南瓜哟！

詹姆士：我可能得带上阿莱克斯，可以吗？

艾玛：当然了，没问题的。

克丽斯滕：那我们明晚见吧！

威尔、詹姆士：明晚见！

（女孩子从舞台右边下台，男孩子从左边下台。）

Scene 3: Emma's House

(The table has pumpkins, plates with snacks, and some water bottles. Emma, Kyrsten, and Will are center stage.)

Will: *(Eating a cupcake.)* These cupcakes are great!

Kyrsten: They're supposed to be for dessert, Will!

Will: I like eating dessert first!

Emma: And second and third.

Will: I love cupcakes.

Kyrsten: Just save some for the rest of us.

Will: You snooze; you lose! It's not my fault if you miss out.

(James and Alex enter stage right. James is carrying a bag. Alex has two small pumpkins.)

Emma: Hi, guys! I'm glad you could come!

James: Thanks for inviting us! My mom sent fruit with dip and some huge chocolate chip cookies.

Will: Mmm, cookies? Let's see! *(Takes the bag and pulls out a cookie.)*

Alex: *(Grabs the bag.)* Give me one, too!

James: *(Taking the bag back.)* You've had enough, Alex! You ate two in the car!

Alex: Do you have any gummy worms?

James: *(Rolls his eyes.)* No, Alex! They don't have gummy worms.

(Alex pouts.)

(Emma and Kyrsten talk quietly with Alex.)

James: *(Pointing to Will's costume.)* You know, Will, it isn't Halloween yet.

Will: I know that! I just decided I needed the practice putting together my costume.

James: *(Laughing.)* Well you don't see a mummy eating a cupcake and carving a pumpkin every day, that's for sure!

Will: *(Laughing.)* If I need a napkin, I'm all set!

James: Guess what I saw on the way over?

Will: *(Munching on a cookie.)* I don't know. What?

James: There were lights on in the old Miller mansion again!

(Emma moves over next to James.)

Emma: Did you see them, too? My mom said there were lights on when she went past on her way home from work.

Kyrsten: That's really creepy. It's been empty for as long as I can remember. Maybe it really *is* haunted!

Emma: Anyone want to go exploring tonight?

Will: Not me! I was invited to carve pumpkins and eat. That's what I came for.

Kyrsten: I really don't want to see any ghosts, Emma!

James: I'll go!

Alex: Me, too!

James: (*Shaking his head.*) You can't go. You're too little.

Emma: I think it would be cool if the Miller mansion is haunted! That house is over 200 years old. I bet some amazing things have happened there.

James: (*Rubbing his hands together.*) And October's a good time for ghost hunting. It's only three more days until Halloween.

Will: (*Sits down and folds his arms over his chest.*) I don't want any part of this!

Kyrsten: Me, either!

Emma: I guess we'd better just carve our pumpkins tonight, James.

James: (*Whispering.*) But maybe we could take a look at the mansion when I take Alex trick-or-treating Friday night! Will and I were going to dress up anyway.

Emma: (*Whispering back.*) Kyrsten and I are, too! That's a great idea. I'll talk to you about it later!

第三幕：艾玛家

（桌子上放着南瓜、盛有零食的餐盘和几瓶水。艾玛、克丽斯滕和威尔在舞台中央。）

威尔：(吃着纸杯蛋糕) 这些纸杯蛋糕真好吃！

克丽斯滕：这可是饭后甜点，威尔！

威尔：我的前餐就是饭后甜点！

艾玛：然后正餐还是饭后甜点，再然后，就停不下来了。

威尔：我最爱纸杯蛋糕了。

克丽斯滕：也给我们留点啊。

威尔：你晚了一步，机会错过啦！是你自己太慢了，不是我的错哟！

（詹姆士和阿莱克斯从舞台右边上台。詹姆士背个大包，阿莱克斯拎着两个小南瓜。）

艾玛：嘿，朋友们！你们来了，我太高兴了！

詹姆士：谢谢你的邀请！我妈妈给我带了水果和蘸酱，还有一些巧克力仁曲奇饼干。

威尔：哇，曲奇饼干？让我看看！（接过书包，拿出饼干）

阿莱克斯：（抢过书包）也给我一块！

詹姆士：（抢回书包）阿莱克斯，够了！你在车里就吃了两块了！

阿莱克斯：你们有没有橡皮虫啊？

詹姆士：（翻白眼）好了，阿莱克斯！他们没有橡皮虫！（阿莱克斯噘起嘴）

（艾玛和克丽斯滕同阿莱克斯轻声交谈。）

詹姆士：（指着威尔的服饰）嗨，威尔，现在还不是万圣节呢。

威尔：我知道呀！我只想提前适应一下这身衣服。

詹姆士：（大笑）好吧。吃纸杯蛋糕、刻南瓜的木乃伊不是每天都有的，这个我敢肯定。

威尔：（大笑）再给我一张餐巾纸的话，我万圣节的服饰就齐了！

詹姆士：你们猜，我来这儿的路上看到什么了？

威尔：（大口嚼着饼干）猜不出来，看到什么了？

詹姆士：老米勒的洋楼里又有灯光了！

（艾玛走到詹姆士旁边。）

艾玛：你也看到灯光了？我妈妈说，她下班回来经过那儿时，也看到了灯光。

克丽斯滕：这可有点儿恐怖。自打我记事起，那房子就一直空着了。没准，里面有幽灵！

艾玛：有没有人想今晚去探险？

威尔：我可不去！我来是因为你们请我来刻南瓜、吃夜宵的。

克丽斯滕：艾玛，我也不想看到幽灵什么的！

詹姆士：我去！

阿莱克斯：我也去！

詹姆士：（摇着头说）你不能去。你还太小了。

艾玛：要是老米勒的洋楼里有幽灵，那挺酷的！这房子有200年了。我猜，那儿一定发生过什么不可思议的事情。

詹姆士：（搓着手）十月是抓鬼的最佳时机。离万圣节只剩下三天了。

威尔：（坐下，双手抱在胸前）我不想参与这个！

克丽斯滕：我也不想！

艾玛：詹姆士，我想，咱们今晚还是好好刻南瓜吧。

詹姆士：(小声说)或者，周五晚上我带阿莱克斯去讨糖果的时候，咱们去看看那个洋楼！我和威尔至少化了妆，不怕的。

艾玛：(小声回答)克丽斯滕和我也会化妆的！这是个好主意。我俩一会儿好好说下计划。

Scene 4: Halloween Night

(Turn the lights out. Emma, Will, and Kyrsten walk down the center aisle toward the stage. They are carrying flashlights and trick-or-treating bags.)

Will: It's windy tonight.

Kyrsten: And cold, too. It's kind of spooky out here with all the bare trees.

Emma: And look, Kyrsten! The moon is full! *(Howling.)* Owwwoooo!

Kyrsten: Stop that!

Alex: *(Walks on from stage right. James is following him. Both are wearing their costumes.)* Thanks for the popcorn! *(Alex waves to someone offstage.)*

James: You have a ton of candy. Are you ready to quit?

Alex: No way! I'm just getting started.

Emma: Look, James! Do you see what I see?

(Stage crew shines a light from stage left.)

James: Cool! There's a light in the Miller mansion tonight!

Will: Okay, I'm done if you guys are planning to go down there.

Emma: James and I thought we'd just walk by it. And maybe peek in the windows.

Kyrsten: Then I'm going home!

Emma: You can't walk home alone, Kyrsten. All we want to do is have a look around. I promise we won't go in.

Kyrsten: I'm staying right here on the sidewalk with Will. You and James can look around.

Emma: *(Rolls her eyes.)* Fine with me!

Alex: *(Spins around in his costume and sings.)* I love candy! I love candy!

James: *(Grabs Alex.)* Okay, you're cut off.

Alex: I only ate ten candy bars!

James: *(Slaps his hand to his forehead.)* Oh, Alex! Mom will never let me take you trick-or-treating again! You're supposed to wait until we get home to eat anything. Stay here with Will and Kyrsten. Emma and I will be right back.

Alex: I want to see the ghost! I'm coming with you.

Emma: No, you're not, Alex.

Alex: I am! I am! I am! *(Runs toward the Miller mansion and then falls down.)*

Owww! *(Alex starts to cry.)*

James: *(Running after Alex.)* Oh man, now he got hurt! *(Turn stage or room lights on.)*

Kyrsten: The porch light just came on!

Will: I'd better go help.

Kyrsten: I'll go too! I'm not staying here alone!

Will: The door is opening! Do something!

Kyrsten: What do you want me to do?

James: *(Kneeling down by Alex.)* Come on, Alex! Let's get out of here!

(Miss Craig enters stage left.)

Emma: Wait! Is that . . . ?

Kyrsten: Miss Craig?

Miss Craig: Alex, are you okay?

Alex: I hurt my knee!

James: I don't understand. What are you doing here, Miss Craig?

Miss Craig: *(Laughing.)* I live here! This was my grandfather's house.

James: So you've been turning the lights on at night?

Miss Craig: Well, it *is* hard to see at night without any lights. Why don't you all come inside and I'll explain. I need to find a Band-Aid for Alex's knee. You can have some cookies and hot chocolate.

Emma, **Kyrsten**, **Will**, & **James:** *(Looking at each other.)* Sure!

第四幕：万圣节的晚上

（关掉舞台的灯光。艾玛、威尔和克丽斯滕从观众席的过道上台。他们手里拿着手电筒和讨糖果用的小布袋。）

威尔：今晚风够大的。

克丽斯滕：而且还挺冷的。那些光秃秃的树看起来挺瘆人的。

艾玛：看，克丽斯滕，月圆了！（学狼叫）嗷呜——！

克丽斯滕：别这样！

阿莱克斯：（阿莱克斯从舞台右侧上台。詹姆士跟在其后。两个人都穿着万圣节服饰）。谢谢您的爆米花！（阿莱克斯向台下挥手。）

詹姆士：你已经有一大堆糖了。要不回家吧？

阿莱克斯：才不呢！我刚开始玩呢！

艾玛：詹姆士，你看！你看见我说的了吗？

（舞台工作人员在左侧发出灯光。）

詹姆士：太酷了！今晚老米勒的洋房里也有光！

威尔：好了，你们要是想去那儿，我就退出。

艾玛：詹姆士和我之前打算，咱们就路过那儿一下。或许，再从窗户往里看一眼。

克丽斯滕：那我回家了！

艾玛：克丽斯滕，你不能自己回去。我们只不过去看一下。我保证，我们不进去。

克丽斯滕：我和威尔待在人行道这儿。你和詹姆士可以过去看一下。

艾玛：（翻白眼）我没问题！

阿莱克斯：（穿着他的服装边唱边转来转去。）我爱糖果！我爱糖果！

詹姆士：（抓住阿莱克斯）好吧。不许再吃这些糖果了。

阿莱克斯：我只吃了五根糖果棒！

詹姆士：（拍自己的前额）天哪，阿莱克斯！妈妈一定不会再让我带你去讨糖果了！你应该等到我们回到家后，吃完饭再吃甜点的。你跟克丽斯滕和威尔待在这儿。艾玛和我马上就回来。

阿莱克斯：我想去看幽灵！我跟你一起去。

艾玛：阿莱克斯，你不可以跟我们一起去。

阿莱克斯：我就去！就去！就去！（跑向老米勒洋楼，然后跌倒）哎哟！（阿莱克斯哭起来。）

詹姆士：（跑向阿莱克斯）天哪，他摔倒了！

（舞台或者洋楼里的灯亮了）

克丽斯滕：门廊的灯亮了！

威尔：我得去帮他们。

克丽斯滕：我也去！我不想自己待在这儿！

威尔：门开了！咱们得做点儿什么了！

克丽斯滕：你想让我做什么？

詹姆士：（跪在阿莱克斯旁边）快，阿莱克斯！咱们得离开这儿！

（克蕾格老师从舞台左侧上台）

艾玛：等一下！这不是……？

克蕾格老师：哦，阿莱克斯，你没事吧？

阿莱克斯：我磕到膝盖了！

詹姆士：我有点儿糊涂了。克蕾格老师，您在这房子里做什么呀？

克蕾格老师：（大笑）我住在这儿啊！这是我祖父的房子。

詹姆士：所以，是您每天晚上开的灯？

克蕾格老师：对呀，没灯晚上怎么看得见啊。你们都先进来吧，然后，我再给你们讲我的事儿。我得给阿莱克斯找创可贴。你们可以吃点儿巧克力饼干配热可可。

艾玛、詹姆士、威尔、克丽斯滕：（相互看看）太好啦！

Scene 5: The Mansion

(Everyone is onstage. There is a table with mugs and cookies.)

Emma: So, you moved here from California because your grandfather died?

Miss Craig: Yes, he had been in a nursing home for a long time.

Kyrsten: None of us ever remember anyone living here. It's always been empty.

Miss Craig: Well, I always loved this house. I used to visit it when I was a little girl. Then last year when my grandfather died, he left it to me in his will.

Will: It's a big house for one person.

Miss Craig: It is a big house, but I really want to fix it up. There's a lot to do. I hired Emma's dad to be my contractor.

Emma: I didn't know that!

James: So that's why the yellow tape was up on Tuesday.

Miss Craig: Yes, they're putting in a new sidewalk. I think that's why Alex tripped. I hadn't turned on my porch light because the front yard isn't safe for trick-or-treating.

James: Well, Alex is kind of a klutz. *And* he's had way too much sugar tonight.

Alex: *(Jumping up and down.)* Do you have any gummy worms?

Miss Craig: No, Alex. I'm sorry, I don't!

Alex: Can I have another cookie?

James: No!

(Alex crawls under the table.)

Miss Craig: Why did all of you look so startled when I opened the door?

Kyrsten: We thought your house was haunted.

Miss Craig: Well, if it is, they must be very happy

ghosts! This house was always filled with laughter when I was little. I have such good memories of spending my summers here.

Emma: Well, so much for ghost hunting!

James: Yeah, there's always next year. I really wanted to see a ghost!

Alex: *(Crawls out from under the table with the tablecloth over his head.)* Ooooooo!

The End

第五幕：洋楼

（全体演员都在台上。桌子上摆着杯子和曲奇饼干）

艾玛：所以，因为您的祖父去世了，您才从加利福尼亚搬到这儿？

克蕾格老师：是的。他在养老院住了很长时间了。

克丽斯滕：这房子里还住过人，我们真的一点印象都没有了。这房子一直都空着。

克蕾格老师：说实话，我一直都很喜欢这栋房子。小的时候，我常常来这儿拜访祖父。去年，他去世时，在遗嘱里，他把这栋房子留给了我。

威尔：这房子要是一个人住，真的挺大的。

克蕾格老师：是的，我很想把它好好修整一下。要做的事儿还挺多的。我请了艾玛的爸爸来担任我的承包商。

艾玛：这件事我一点儿都不知道！

詹姆士：哦，所以从周二起，才会有那些隔离带。

克蕾格老师：对的，他们正在重修一条人行道。我估计，这就是为什么阿莱克斯刚才被绊倒了。因为前院在施工，请小朋友们来讨糖果不太安全，所以，我没开门廊的灯。

詹姆士：没事的，阿莱克斯就是个傻瓜。今晚他吃了太多的糖，就更傻了。

阿莱克斯：（上蹿下跳）您有没有橡皮糖？

克蕾格老师：噢，阿莱克斯，很抱歉，我没有那个！

阿莱克斯：我能再吃块饼干吗？

詹姆士：不可以了！

（阿莱克斯在桌下爬来爬去）

克蕾格老师：我开门的时候，你们怎么都那么慌张啊？

克丽斯滕：因为我们还以为这栋房子里有幽灵呢。

克蕾格老师：哈哈，要是有的话，也是快乐的幽灵！自打我小时候起，这栋房子就充满了欢声笑语。我记忆里的每个暑假，都是那么的幸福。

艾玛：好吧，抓鬼行动到这儿就结束啦！

詹姆士：对，明年还可以再来。我真的想看看幽灵！

阿莱克斯：（从桌下爬出，头顶着桌布）嗷呜！

全剧终

故事剧场二

火鸡大餐和打包外卖

布景

第一幕发生在室外。用几棵画好的树做背景。这一幕也可以用拉上的大幕做背景，这样，舞台工作人员就可以轻松地为第二幕做准备了。

第二幕发生在马蒂的厨房里，所以背景要有水池、橱柜和碗柜。另外，再放一张餐桌和三把椅子。

第三幕发生在祖父家里。背景为：小沙发、地毯和茶几。

第四幕发生在流浪者之家。用两张长桌子来放食物。两张桌子需要对着放，一个在舞台左侧，一个在右侧。

第五幕发生在流浪者之家的后院。用硬纸板做出院墙。然后，把一个便携式篝火炉摆在舞台上，里面可以放橘红色的纸片充当篝火，这样演员就可以围在两边假装烤棉花糖了。

道具

- ☐ 大竹筐
- ☐ 一盘曲奇饼干
- ☐ 一次性锡纸餐具
- ☐ 耙子
- ☐ 一杯牛奶
- ☐ 塑料叶子
- ☐ 碗
- ☐ 锡纸
- ☐ 盘子

- ☐ 几个大锅
- ☐ 烤棉花糖用的木棍
- ☐ 银餐具
- ☐ 餐勺
- ☐ 杂志
- ☐ 几碗土豆泥
- ☐ 棉花糖
- ☐ 咖啡杯
- ☐ 餐巾纸

演员表

马蒂·邓肯: 超喜欢过感恩节的小女孩

祖父: 马蒂的祖父

塔拉: 马蒂的朋友

马申先生: 流浪者之家的负责人

邓肯女士: 马蒂的妈妈

邓肯先生: 马蒂的爸爸

群演1: 感恩节来流浪者之家领饭的人

群演2: 感恩节来流浪者之家领饭的人

群演3: 丹尼叔叔，马蒂的叔叔

妆容和服装

大部分的演员可以穿生活装上台表演。只有如下的演员，需要特殊服装或配饰：

丹尼叔叔：帽衫和火鸡配饰。

祖父：用眉笔画出"皱纹"，还要配上假胡须和光头头套。

排演安排和舞台方位

舞台左侧

上舞台中心

舞台正位

下舞台中心

舞台右侧

←--- 左侧幕区

右侧幕区 --→

Script: Turkey and Takeout

Scene 1: Outside Tara's House

(Maddy and Tara need a basket and a rake. Scatter artificial colored leaves around the stage. The girls should pick up and rake the leaves and put them in the basket as they are talking. Use a tree backdrop or stand-up fake trees.)

Maddy: I love Thanksgiving! I'm so glad it's next week!

Tara: *(Throws little handfuls of leaves into the air.)* Turkey, mashed potatoes, and pumpkin pie! Yum!

Maddy: You should try my grandpa's mashed potatoes. I think he uses cream cheese!

Tara: My grandma makes awesome pumpkin pie and apple pie.

Maddy: We always have apple pie, too, and sometimes pecan pie. My dad loves that.

Tara: *(Makes a face.)* Ick! Too many nuts.

Maddy: After dinner, my uncle Danny makes up a treasure hunt for all the kids. We get clues that take us all over the house and even outside. Whoever finds the

treasure first gets to keep it. Last year, I won!

Tara: That sounds like more fun than doing dishes. I always get stuck helping with those. Everyone else at my house hangs out in the living room, snoring and watching football.

Maddy: We all go for a walk when the dishes are done. It's usually a little cold. One year we even had snow flurries! When we come back, Daddy lights a fire in the fireplace and we make s'mores, pop popcorn, and tell stories.

Tara: Okay, the Duncans win the Family of the Year award! That sounds so nice. Can I come to your house for Thanksgiving?

Maddy: Sure! That would be fun!

Tara: Just kidding. I'd really like to, but my mom would be upset. My family likes to have everything just the same every year. It's tradition and all that. *(Rolls her eyes.)*

Maddy: I know what you mean. My family is that way,

too. It's kind of nice, though. I look forward to it every year. If something changed, it just wouldn't be the same!

Mrs. Duncan: *(Calling from offstage.)* Maddy! Are you almost finished? Dinner's ready!

Maddy: I'd better go.

Tara: I can finish this.

Maddy: *(Throws a handful of leaves at Tara.)* See you tomorrow!

剧本：火鸡大餐和打包外卖

第一幕：塔拉家外面

（马蒂和塔拉需要一个筐和耙子。舞台上布满散落的塑料叶子。女孩子们一边聊天，一边把这些叶子捡起来，把叶子耙清，再把落叶放在筐里。背景可以放棵真树，也可以放棵假树。）

马蒂：我太爱过感恩节了！下周就是了，真高兴！

塔拉：(抓起一把落叶，抛向空中) 一过节，就会有火鸡、土豆泥，还有南瓜饼！好吃极啦！

马蒂：你得尝尝我祖父做的土豆泥。他好像往里面加了奶油芝士酱呢！

塔拉：我祖母做的南瓜饼和苹果派也棒棒的。

马蒂：我们那天也会有苹果派的，有时，还会有山核桃饼。我爸爸最爱吃这个了。

塔拉：(做个鬼脸) 呃！太多坚果了。

马蒂：吃完饭，我叔叔丹尼会带所有的孩子去找宝藏。我们按照得到的线索在整栋房子里找，也会去外面找呢。谁第一个找到宝藏，谁就可以拥有它。去年，我是第一名哟！

塔拉：这个可比洗碗有意思多了。我总得帮忙收拾。别人就可以去客厅休息啊、睡觉啊，或者去看足球比赛。

马蒂：收拾完碗筷，我们全家会一起去散步。每年感恩节那会儿，天就凉了。有一年散步时，还下雪了呢！回到家，爸爸就会把篝火升起来，我们一起做些篝火甜点①、爆米花，还讲故事什么的。

塔拉：好吧，邓肯一家获"今年最幸福家庭奖"！你家的感恩节好有意思。今年我能去你家过吗？

马蒂：当然了！你来的话，肯定会更有意思的！

塔拉：开玩笑啦。我是挺想去的，不过，我妈妈会伤心的。我家习惯年年都做同样的事。他们说，这是传统。（翻白眼）

马蒂：我懂你。我家其实也是这样的。只不过，我们的传统挺有意思的。每年，我都特别期待这一天的到

————————————

① 美国、加拿大等地篝火甜点的做法：全麦饼干夹一层巧克力和烤软的棉花糖。

来。要是有什么小变动，那可就不是传统了！

邓肯女士：(从台下喊)马蒂！你扫完了吗？晚饭好啦！

马蒂：我得走了。

塔拉：我可以把它干完。

马蒂：(向塔拉抛枯叶)明天见喽！

Scene 2: Maddy's Kitchen

(Set the stage with a table and three chairs. A painted backdrop should show a sink, a counter, and cupboards. Mrs. Duncan is putting plates on the table. Maddy enters from stage right.)

Mrs. Duncan: Hi, honey! Wash your hands, and then could you set the table for me?

Maddy: Sure! *(Maddy pretends to wash her hands at the sink.)*

Mrs. Duncan: Did you get the leaves in Tara's yard raked?

Maddy: Some of them. We were mostly throwing them around.

Mrs. Duncan: *(She hands Maddy some silverware.)* Well it sounds like you had fun!

Maddy: We were talking about Thanksgiving. *(She spins around and hugs herself.)* I *love* Thanksgiving!

Mrs. Duncan: *(Stops and hesitates.)* This year, Thanksgiving will be especially awesome!

Maddy: *(Stops twirling and sounds puzzled.)* Why? What's going to be different?

Mrs. Duncan: We're volunteering at the homeless shelter on Fifth Street.

Maddy: *(Staring at her mother.)* Who's volunteering?

Mrs. Duncan: You and Daddy and I! We're going to serve dinner all day to people who wouldn't have a Thanksgiving meal otherwise.

Maddy: *(Angrily.)* Why didn't you tell me? You didn't even ask me if I wanted to do that!

Mrs. Duncan: I'm sorry, honey. I didn't think I needed to. Daddy and I just decided last night. We were going to tell you tonight at dinner. I thought you would be excited to have a chance to help other people.

Maddy: *(Puts silverware down and folds her arms over*

her chest.) I *do* want to help other people . . . just not on Thanksgiving.

Mrs. Duncan: (*Sounding offended.*) Maddy! Some people in our town don't have enough to eat. Do you want Thanksgiving to be just another day for them? Daddy and I thought this would be such a good way to give something back to the community.

Maddy: (*In a very soft voice.*) But I love Thanksgiving, Mom. I don't want it to be different this year. I want to have Thanksgiving dinner with just our family. I want Grandpa's mashed potatoes and your pumpkin pie. I want s'mores and stories and Uncle Danny's treasure hunt.

Mrs. Duncan: Maddy, it isn't as though Thanksgiving celebrations have always remained the same. At the first Thanksgiving celebration in Plymouth, they didn't have mashed potatoes or cranberry sauce or pumpkin pie. There may not even have been turkey.

Maddy: No turkey?

Mrs. Duncan: No, they had venison, which is deer meat. They were giving thanks for their first good harvest after not having enough to eat the year before. They invited the Wampanoag with their chief, Massasoit, to celebrate with them because they appreciated their help. Maddy, our Thanksgiving, which you love so much, isn't really traditional. Most people don't make s'mores or have a goofy uncle who plans Thanksgiving treasure hunts!

Maddy: I know Tara doesn't. She wanted to come to our house because our Thanksgiving sounded like so much fun.

Mrs. Duncan: Helping at the homeless shelter will be fun, too.

Maddy: But, it won't be the same!

Mrs. Duncan: No, it won't be the same. But it can still be a very nice holiday. Think how good you'll feel to be helping people. And you'll still be with your dad and me.

Maddy: *(Angrily.)* What if I hate it? What if Thanksgiving is *awful*? *(She exits stage right.)*

Mrs. Duncan: Maddy, come back! Daddy will be home in five minutes and dinner is ready.

Maddy: *(Yelling from offstage.)* I'm not hungry!

第二幕：马蒂家的厨房

（舞台所需道具为一张桌子和三把椅子。背景是水池、橱柜和碗柜。邓肯女士正在摆桌子。马蒂从舞台右侧上台。）

邓肯女士：哎，亲爱的！先去洗手，然后，你来帮我摆桌子，好吗？

马蒂：好的！（马蒂做出在水池洗手的样子）

邓肯女士：你今天把塔拉院子里的叶子都扫干净了吗？

马蒂：只收拾完了一部分。我们大多数时间在忙着打叶子仗呢。

邓肯女士：（递给马蒂一些银餐具）你们玩得挺开心啊！

马蒂：我们聊了聊感恩节。（她转来转去，然后，双手抱臂）我太爱过感恩节了！

邓肯女士：（停下手中的活，犹豫一下）今年的感恩节，会特别有意义！

马蒂：（不再转了，神秘地说）为什么，会有什么不一样的吗？

邓肯女士：今年的感恩节，我们要去第五街区流浪者之家做志愿者。

马蒂：（盯着妈妈）谁去做志愿者？

邓肯女士：你爸爸、你和我。那天我们要去照顾那些吃不上感恩节大餐的人们。

马蒂：（生气）你为什么之前不告诉我呢？你都没问我想不想参加！

邓肯女士：哦，对不起，亲爱的。我不觉得我得先征求你的同意。你爸爸和我昨晚做了这个决定。我们是打算吃晚饭的时候告诉你的。我还以为，你会特别期待这个可以帮助别人的机会呢。

马蒂：（放下银餐具，生气地抱臂）我不想帮助别人……至少，不想在感恩节做这个。

邓肯女士：（声音有点儿生气）马蒂！我们镇上有人连饭都吃不上。你不想给他们一个特殊的感恩节吗？你爸爸和我都觉得，帮助这些人是咱们对这个社区最好的回报。

马蒂：（弱弱地说）妈妈，可是……我特别期待过感恩节。我不想过得和往年不一样。我只想和自己家人吃感恩节大餐。我想吃祖父做的土豆泥和你做的南瓜饼。我想吃篝火甜点、听故事，还想和丹尼叔叔找宝藏。

邓肯女士：马蒂，并不是咱们每年过感恩节的方式都一样呀。我们的祖先第一次在普利茅斯庆祝感恩节的时候，他们连土豆泥或者果蔓酱都没有，更别提南瓜饼了。他们甚至连火鸡都没有。

马蒂：连火鸡都没有？

邓肯女士：没有。但是，他们有些野味，是鹿肉大餐。他们用这些食物来感恩第一次大丰收。在那之前，我们的祖先连饭都吃不上呢。为了对万帕诺亚格的印第安人和他们的首领马萨索德表示感谢，我们的祖先邀请了当地人一同庆贺。马蒂，咱家感恩节的习惯，也就是你最喜欢的这些节目，并不是真正的传统。大多数人都不会在这天做篝火甜点，更不会像你叔叔那样，异想天开地玩什么寻宝！

马蒂：我知道，塔拉她家就不像咱们这么庆祝。她还想来咱们家过感恩节呢，她觉得咱们家的更有意思。

邓肯女士：在流浪者之家做志愿者也会很有意思。

马蒂：但是，这和每年我们过的感恩节就不一样了！

邓肯女士：对，是和每年的不一样。不过，这仍然会是个有意义的节日。设想一下，你自己助人为乐后的那种满足感吧。而且，整个节日，你都会跟爸爸和我一起庆祝。

马蒂：（生气地）要是我讨厌助人为乐呢？要是今年的感恩节对我来说，糟糕透顶呢？（她从舞台右边下台）

邓肯女士：马蒂，回来！五分钟之内，爸爸就要到家了，咱们的晚饭已经好了。

马蒂：（在台下大喊）我一点儿都不饿！

Scene 3: Grandpa's House

(Use a rug, a small sofa, and a side table or coffee table to set the scene. Put a plate of cookies on the coffee table. Grandpa sits in a chair reading a magazine and drinking coffee.)

(Maddy knocks from offstage. Grandpa gets up to open the door.)

Maddy: Hi, Grandpa.

Grandpa: *(Gives her a hug.)* Hi, Maddy!

Maddy: I asked Mom if I could stop by on my way home from school. She knows I'm here.

Grandpa: I know, she called me. She just wanted to make sure I would be home when you stopped by. I'm going to volunteer at the library at four o'clock, but that leaves a whole hour just for you! Come and sit down.

(Maddy follows him in but doesn't say anything else.)

Grandpa: *(Points at the coffee table.)* How about a glass of milk to go with these cookies?

Maddy: Okay. I do love pumpkin cookies.

(Grandpa exits stage left. He returns with a glass of milk and sets it on the coffee table.)

Grandpa: Is there something you'd like to talk about, Maddy?

Maddy: *(Nods her head.)* I want to talk about Thanksgiving. Mom said we're helping at the homeless shelter this year.

Grandpa: That's a really nice thing to do.

Maddy: I know it is, but I feel like it's going to ruin *our* Thanksgiving.

Grandpa: It's going to make a lot of people very happy.

Maddy: Not me. I'll miss your mashed potatoes and Mom's pie and just being together with everyone. It won't be the same.

Grandpa: I'll tell you something funny, Maddy. It's the

holidays that are different that people remember best. All the ones that are the same kind of blend together.

Maddy: What do you mean?

Grandpa: Do you remember the year Uncle Danny dropped his marshmallow and set the rug on fire?

Maddy: *(Laughing.)* Yes! Daddy had to use the fire extinguisher!

Grandpa: And how about the year the treasure was a dozen giant gingerbread cookies and the dog gobbled them up before you found them?

Maddy: I remember that, too! All that was left was a slobbery bag. There weren't even any crumbs!

Grandpa: And how about two years ago when it snowed and the roads were so bad no one could drive home?

Maddy: All the kids slept on the living room floor and Uncle Danny told us ghost stories all night.

Grandpa: So every Thanksgiving hasn't been the same, has it?

Maddy: I guess not. But they were all fun!

Grandpa: That's right! They *were* all fun. And this one will be fun, too. Promise.

第三幕：祖父的家

　　（屋内的布置为一块地毯、一个小沙发、一个茶几或者小桌子。桌子上放着盛满饼干的盘子。祖父坐在椅子上边看杂志，边喝咖啡。）

（马蒂从台下敲门。祖父起身开门。）

马蒂：你好，祖父。

祖父：（拥抱马蒂）噢，我的马蒂！

马蒂：我问了妈妈，放学后可不可以来看看您。所以，她应该知道我在您这儿。

祖父：对，她跟我通过话了。她之前想知道，你放学路过我这儿的时候，家里有没有人。我下午四点才去图书馆服务，所以，这一个小时的时间就属于你和我了！来坐下吧。

（马蒂进来，跟在他身后，可是她什么也没说）

祖父：（指着咖啡桌）要不要吃点儿曲奇饼干，再配杯牛奶？

马蒂：好呀。我最喜欢曲奇饼干了。

(祖父从舞台左侧下台。再上台时，手里拿着一杯牛奶，他把牛奶放在咖啡桌上。)

祖父：马蒂，你是不是有什么事想告诉我呢？

马蒂：(点点头)我想跟您聊聊感恩节。妈妈说，今年的感恩节，我们要在流浪者之家做志愿者。

祖父：这可是个好主意呀。

马蒂：好吧。可是，我觉得今年的感恩节一定会糟糕透顶的。

祖父：不会的，今年的感恩节会给更多的人带来快乐。

马蒂：不会给我带来快乐的。我会想死您的土豆泥和妈妈的南瓜饼，还有和咱家人在一起的感觉。今年的感恩节不会像往年那么快乐的。

祖父：让我来给你讲点儿有趣的事儿吧，我的马蒂。其实，每年过节，发生的那些不同寻常的事情，才会让人们念念不忘呢。那些年年重复的片段，反而记不清了。

马蒂：什么意思呢？

祖父：你还记得那年，丹尼叔叔把他的棉花糖掉在了毯子上，结果小毯子着火了吗？

马蒂:(大笑)当然记得!我爸爸还用了灭火器呢!

祖父:还有那年,就是你们找姜饼宝藏的那年,在你们找到之前,狗狗把它都吃光了。

马蒂:我记得呢!我们只找到了满是口水的破袋子,干净得连渣儿都没给我们剩。

祖父:还记得两年前吗?那场雪下得这么大,人们连车都开不了了。

马蒂:所有的孩子都得睡在客厅,丹尼叔叔给我们讲了整晚鬼故事呢。

祖父：所以，每年的感恩节都不一样，对吗？

马蒂：对的。但是，每年的感恩节都那么有意思！

祖父：是的！每年的感恩节，我们都过得那么有意义。今年也会这样的。我向你保证。

Scene 4: The Homeless Shelter

(Set the stage with two long tables with big pots, bowls, pie pans, and paper plates. Have two other tables set diagonally with tablecloths and silverware, one stage right and one stage left.)

(Maddy enters from stage right with her parents. Mrs. Duncan carries a box of pies.)

Mr. Marsh: Happy Thanksgiving! Thank you so much for coming along to help, Maddy.

Maddy: Happy Thanksgiving, Mr. Marsh.

Grandpa: *(Enters from stage left with a huge bowl of mashed potatoes.)* Happy Thanksgiving, all!

Maddy: Grandpa! What are you doing here? Why didn't you tell me you were coming?

Grandpa: I made the mashed potatoes. And I wanted to

surprise you!

Maddy: *(Gives him a hug.)* I'm really glad you're here! *(Several people walk in from stage right.)*

Mr. Marsh: It looks like people are ready to eat. Mr. Duncan, can you cut the pies and cakes and put them on paper plates? Then I'd love some help carving these turkeys.

Mr. Duncan: Sure! *(Goes over to the serving table.)*

Mr. Marsh: Mrs. Duncan, would you serve the corn and green beans?

Mrs. Duncan: I'd be glad to!

Grandpa: Maddy, you can serve the potatoes. And don't be stingy. There are plenty more in the kitchen.

Maddy: Okay!

Mr. Marsh: Let's get busy! And be sure to make everyone feel welcome.

(The first people approach Maddy carrying plates, and Maddy pretends to serve them.)

Maddy: Happy Thanksgiving! Would you like some

mashed potatoes?

Person 1: Yes, please.

Maddy: Hello! Do you like mashed potatoes? My grandpa made them. They're so good!

Person 2: Thank you very much!

(Person 3 approaches with a turkey costume on. The hood hides most of his face.)

Maddy: *(Starts to laugh.)* Happy Thanksgiving, Mr. Turkey! Do you like mashed potatoes?

Person 3: Do you do takeout?

Maddy: Takeout? I don't know. Mr. Marsh, can we do takeout for this turkey?

Mr. Marsh: *(Laughing.)* Why not? How many meals do you need?

Person 3: *(Pulls down his hood.)* I'm just kidding, Maddy. It's me!

Maddy: Uncle Danny! I can't believe you came!

Uncle Danny: Well, this is where my family is. I think I should help, too. What can I do?

Mr. Marsh: Can you take over serving the stuffing? I'll go and greet people!

Uncle Danny: Sure thing! Then I'll be right beside my favorite niece! *(Leans over to Maddy and speaks in a stage whisper.)* Guess what! I thought maybe we could get all the kids to participate in a treasure hunt after

dinner. I brought a nice treasure with me.

Maddy: Really?

Uncle Danny: Of course! It's tradition. And that's the kind of thing favorite uncles do. And I'm your favorite uncle, right?

Maddy: *(Smiling.)* Yes, you are!

第四幕：流浪者之家

（舞台上摆放着四张桌子，两张长桌子上摆着大锅、碗、平锅和纸盘子。两张桌子都用桌布装饰着，上面摆着银器，对着放，一个在舞台左侧，一个在右侧。）

（马蒂和她的父母从舞台右侧上台。邓肯女士抱着一盒馅饼。）

马申先生：感恩节快乐！马蒂，谢谢你的帮助。

马蒂：感恩节快乐，马申先生。

祖父：（从舞台左侧上台，手里捧着一大盆土豆泥）祝大家感恩节快乐！

马蒂：祖父！您在这儿做什么呀？为什么没有告诉我您要来呢？

祖父：哈哈，我做了土豆泥。想给你一个惊喜哟！

马蒂：（拥抱他）您来了，我太高兴了！

（几个人陆续从舞台右侧上台。）

马申先生：看来，大家想开饭了。邓肯先生，你可以切下那些馅饼和蛋糕，再把它们分在纸盘子上吗？要是谁能帮我切下火鸡，我会非常高兴的。

邓肯先生：好的！（走过去上菜）

马申先生：邓肯太太，您能不能发点儿玉米和豌豆粒呢？

邓肯女士：很乐意帮忙！

祖父：马蒂，你可以分点儿土豆泥。别舍不得给哟，厨房里还有一大堆呢。

马蒂：好嘞！

马申先生：大家加油干吧！要让每个人都吃好哟。

（第一个群众演员走近马蒂，手里拿着盘子，马蒂做出盛饭的样子。）

马蒂：感恩节快乐！您想来点儿土豆泥吗？

群演1：好的。

马蒂：您好，您想来点儿土豆泥吗？这是我祖父做的。可好吃了呢！

群演2：好的，非常感谢！

（第三个群众演员慢慢走近，他打扮成一只火鸡。帽子压得低低的，遮住了他的脸。）

马蒂：（笑了起来）感恩节快乐，火鸡先生！您想来点儿土豆泥吗？

群演 3：可不可以打包？

马蒂：打包？这个……我不太清楚。马申先生，我们能不能给这位火鸡先生打包呢？

马申先生：（大笑）当然了！您要打包几份？

群演 3：（摘下帽子）马蒂，我开玩笑呢！你看，是我啊！

马蒂：丹尼叔叔！我真不敢相信，你来了！

丹尼叔叔：当然要来了，我的家人在哪儿我就在哪儿啊。我也想帮忙。我能做点儿什么呢？

马申先生：那你可不可以做招待？我得去接待来宾！

丹尼叔叔：当然可以了！我可以站在我最喜欢的侄女旁边啦！（靠在马蒂旁边，在舞台上轻声交谈。）你猜怎么着，我之前想，吃完饭，咱们没准可以组织所有的孩子来玩寻宝的游戏。我买来了一个特别好的东西当宝藏。

马蒂：真的吗？

丹尼叔叔：当然了！这是咱家的传统嘛。而且，这是咱家马蒂最爱的叔叔的专利呀。我是你最爱的叔叔，对不？

马蒂：（微笑）你是的！

Scene 5: Behind the Homeless Shelter

(Build the outside of the shelter out of cardboard or paint a backdrop. Set the stage with a portable fire pit. Put a string of orange or red lights in it to create a fire-like glow. Make flames out of paper. Have the cast stand around the fire pit in a semicircle, leaving the side toward the audience open.)

Uncle Danny: The fire is ready!

Maddy: Okay, everyone! *(Passing out sticks and marshmallows to the people gathered around.)* Be sure everyone gets a stick and some marshmallows!

(Danny and Maddy move toward stage right as the others roast marshmallows.)

Uncle Danny: So what do you think, Maddy? Was this the Thanksgiving you were dreading?

Maddy: (*Shaking her head.*) No way. I made some new friends. I got to be with my family. We had a great treasure hunt . . .

Uncle Danny: (*Pointing at Maddy.*) Which you could have won but didn't. I saw you hesitate and let that little boy go ahead of you.

Maddy: (*Embarrassed.*) Jake hadn't ever done a treasure hunt before. Did you see how excited he was when he won?

Uncle Danny: I did, and I'm very proud of you. I know you didn't want to do this today.

Maddy: You're right, I didn't. At least, not at first. But this Thanksgiving was very special. It made me feel good.

Uncle Danny: It made me feel good, too!

Maddy: After talking to everyone here, I'm really thankful I have a house and a bed and a family who loves me and . . . (*She stops and smiles.*) Grandpa's mashed potatoes!

Uncle Danny: They really are the best, aren't they? I

think there are still some left in the kitchen. Do you want to go see if we can sneak a bowl of mashed potatoes for takeout?

Maddy: Sure! Happy Thanksgiving, Uncle Danny!

Uncle Danny: Happy Thanksgiving, Maddy!

The End

第五幕：流浪者之家后院

（用硬纸板做出流浪者之家的后院，作为背景。一个篝火炉放在舞台上，里面可以放橘红色的纸片或者红色的灯充当篝火。演员围在篝火炉两边，呈半圆形，面向观众。）

丹尼叔叔：篝火升起来喽！

马蒂：好嘞！（把棉花糖和木棍传给身边的人）每人一个棍子，还有棉花糖哟！

（大家烤棉花糖的时候，丹尼和马蒂挪到舞台右边。）

丹尼叔叔：马蒂，你是不是觉得今年的感恩节糟糕极了？

马蒂：（摇摇头）一点儿都不糟糕。我交了一些新朋友，还跟我的家人一起庆祝，我们又一起找了宝藏……

丹尼叔叔：（指着马蒂）今年的宝藏游戏你本来可以赢的，但是你没争取。我看到你犹豫来着，然后把第一名让给了那个小男孩。

马蒂：（有点儿不好意思）杰克从来没有玩过寻宝游

戏。有没有看到他这次有多兴奋?

丹尼叔叔:看到了,所以我才为你感到骄傲。我知道,你今天不想赢。

马蒂:你说得对,我今天不想赢。至少,不想第一次就赢。今年的感恩节太不一样了,它让我感到幸福。

丹尼叔叔:也让我感到特别幸福!

马蒂：我和每个人都聊了聊他们的家庭。我现在真的很感恩我拥有的一切：一个温暖的家、一张舒服的床、爱我的家人和……（她停顿了一下，向丹尼微笑）和祖父的土豆泥！

丹尼叔叔：那些土豆泥棒极了，是不是？好像厨房还有一些。你想不想试试，偷偷打包带走一碗土豆泥呢？

马蒂：当然想啦！感恩节快乐，亲爱的丹尼叔叔！

丹尼叔叔：感恩节快乐，我的马蒂！

全剧终